Written and Photographed
by Allan Seiden

P9-CJF-050

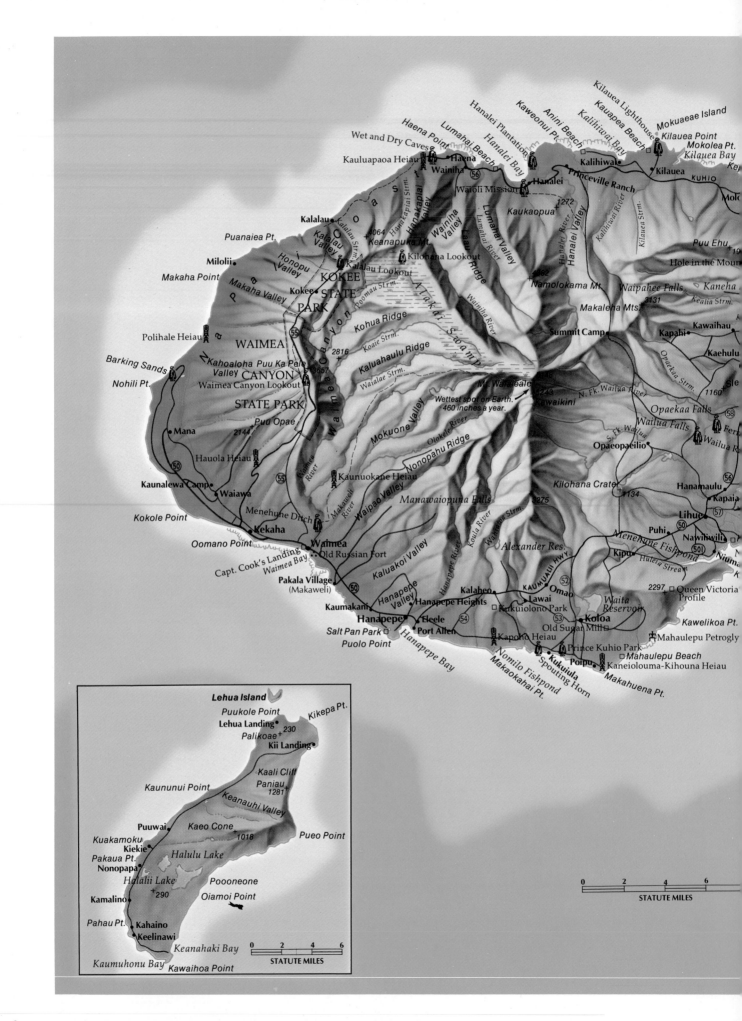

Kilauea Lighthouse
Kaweonui Pt.
Anini Beach
Kalihiwai Beach
Mokuaeae Island
Kauapea Beach
Kilauea Point
Kilauea Lighthouse
Mokolea Pt.
Kilauea Bay
Kauluapaoa Heiau
Wet and Dry Caves
Haena Point
Lumahai Beach
Hanalei Bay
Hanalei Plantation
Mokolea Pt.
Kilauea Bay
Ker
Haena
Wainiha
Kalihiwai
Kilauea
KUHIO
Waioli Mission
Hanalei
Princeville Ranch
Mol
Kalalau
Kalalau
Valley
Keanapura Mt.
Wainiha
Valley
1272
Puu Ehu
Puanaiea Pt.
4064
Lumahai Valley
Kilohana Lookout
Koau Ridge
Lumahai River
Hanalei River
Kalihiwai Strm.
Kilauea Strm.
19
Hole in the Moun
Milolii
Kalalau Lookout
Kalalau Strm.
Hanakapiai Valley
Hanakapiai Strm.
Wainiha River
Namolokama Mt.
Waipahee Falls
Kaneha
Makaha Point
Honopu Valley
KOKEE STATE PARK
Kokee
Makaha Valley
Poomau Strm.
Kohua Ridge
Makaleha Mts.
3131
Kealia Strm.
Kawaihau
Polihale Heiau
WAIMEA CANYON
Kahoaloha
Puu Ka Pele
Valley
2816
Koaie Strm.
Kaluahaulu Ridge
Summit Camp
Opaekaa Strm.
Kapahi
Kaehulu
Barking Sands
3657
Waialae Strm.
Mt. Waialeale
1160
Sle
Nohili Pt.
Waimea Canyon Lookout
Kawaikini
N. Fk. Wailua River
STATE PARK
Wettest spot on Earth. 460 inches a year.
5243
Opaekaa Falls
Puu Opae
Mokuone Valley
Olokele River
Wailua Falls
Wailua
Mana
2144
Nonopahu Ridge
S. Fk. Wailua
Ferr
Hauola Heiau
Opaeopaeilio
Kaunuokane Heiau
Waimea River
Waipao Valley
Manawaiopuna Falls
Koula River
Kilohana Crater
Hanamaulu
Kaunalewa Camp
Waiawa
Menehune Ditch
Makaweli River
3275
134
Kapaia
Kokole Point
Kekaha
Makaweli River
Kaluakoi Valley
Waimea River
Koula River
Waimea Strm.
Alexander Res.
Menehune Fishpond
Lihue
Puhi
Oomano Point
Capt. Cook's Landing
Waimea Bay
Old Russian Fort
Waimea
Hanapepe River
Kaumualii Hwy.
52
Kalaheo
Omao
Kipu
Hulera Stream
Nawiliwili
50
Niuma
501
Pakala Village (Makaweli)
Hanapepe Valley
Hanapepe Heights
Lawai
Kukuiolono Park
Waita Reservoir
2297
Queen Victoria Profile
Kaumakani
Hanapepe
Eleele
Port Allen
54
Koloa
Old Sugar Mill
Kawelikoa Pt.
Salt Pan Park
53
Kapoho Heiau
Nomilo Fishpond
Kukuiula
Mahaulepu Beach
Mahaulepu Petrogly
Puolo Point
Hanapepe Bay
Spouting Horn
Poipu
Kaneiolouma-Kihouna Heiau
Makaokahai Pt.
Prince Kuhio Park
Makahuena Pt.

Lehua Island
Puukole Point
Kikepa Pt.
Lehua Landing
230
Palikoae
Kii Landing
Kaunnunui Point
Kaali Cliff
Paniau
1281
Keanauhi Valley
Puuwai
Kaeo Cone
1018
Pueo Point
Kuakamoku
Kiekie
Pakaua Pt.
Nonopapa
Halulu Lake
Pooooneone
Kamalino
Halalii Lake
290
Oiamoi Point
Pahau Pt.
Kahaino
Keelinawi
Keanahaki Bay
Kaumuhonu Bay
Kawaihoa Point

0   2   4   6
STATUTE MILES

0   2   4   6
STATUTE MILES

y

ua Bay

nahola Bay
Kahala Point
hola

umukumu

alia

aa Beach Park
a

uli
Heiau

k

ark

u Bay

mp
RPORT

h

y

TABLE OF CONTENTS

Kauai: The Garden Isle 4

An Island Is Formed 13

A Lei of Beaches 18

The Menehune 27

An Island Apart 30

Captain Cook: Rendezvous with History 35

Niihau: The Forbidden Island 38

Waimea Canyon: A View from Within 43

South Kauai: The Landscaped Lowlands
  Poipu, Koloa, Lihue, Wailua, and Kapaa 48

Magic & Beauty on the North Shore
  Princeville, Hanalei, and the Na Pali Coast 57

*A rare double rainbow
crowns the Na Pali coastline.*

Kauai

THE GARDEN ISLE

Kauai soothes with a calming softness that is first apparent from the air. Lush fields and valleys flow from dramatically carved mountains. Pasture and forest, taro and sugarcane, smooth rough edges with a completeness that defines Kauai as Hawaii's ultimate garden.

Unlike the other Hawaiian islands, most of Kauai would be green even without man's assistance. The abundant rains that support Waialeale's claim to being the wettest place on earth feed streams that distribute water all around the island. Like the spokes of a wheel, they spill from the forested wilderness of the interior, winding their way through Kauai's valleys and canyons, sometimes moving slowly in deep, calm pools, sometimes pouring over clifftops as thunderous waterfalls.

Opaekaa and Wailua, near Kapaa and Lihue's resorts, are two of the more famous, though many others of equal beauty are to be found. Out toward Princeville and Hanalei water cascades thousands of feet in lacy falls that follow the rains. And along the Na Pali coast these same rains form waterfalls that plunge cliffside into the sea and grace the sheer, green-velvet walls of the larger valleys.

Man has taken his cue from Kauai's lush abundance, planting gardens in visual celebration and studying the broad range of tropical species nurtured by Kauai's ample water and a benign climate with temperatures that range the 70s year-round. From orchids to palms and papaya to sugarcane the tropics bloom profusely on this, Hawaii's Garden Isle.

Plantation agriculture actually got its start on Kauai with the opening of Hawaii's first sugar mill at Koloa in 1835. Sugar is still grown on thousands of irrigated acres along the sunny south coast and processed at mills in Lihue, Koloa, Eleele, and Kekaha. Once there were also expansive fields of pineapple, coffee, tobacco, and rice, but over the years each has been phased out, the victim of cheaper foreign competition. Today with sugar similarly threatened, there is a growing emphasis on tourism, as evidenced by resorts at Poipu, Lihue, Wailua/Kapaa, and Princeville designed to take advantage of Kauai's natural beauty, exceptional beaches, and rural pace.

As on Hawaii's other islands, nineteenth-century plantation agriculture brought with it an influx of immigrant workers to supplement the still-dwindling native Hawaiian population. As had occurred elsewhere, the devastation of disease and the collapse of the old order had depopulated Kauai. Most of those who came to Kauai were Japanese, Filipino or mainland American, providing the island with the distinctive mix that is evident in the exotic features of Kauai's more than 40,000 people.

The Kilauea Lighthouse, adjacent to Kauai's most active bird rookery, is open to visitors. The rookery is protected as a U.S. Fish and Wildlife refuge.

What is perhaps most surprising about Kauai is that it has been so well able to retain its unspoiled beauty and rural lifestyle, despite the pressures of development. The island's mountainous central core, in fact, remains one of Hawaii's most complete wilderness areas, a tribute not only to its inaccessibility, but also to the spiritual impact of the *aina,* the land, that the Hawaiians held sacred.

Much of this natural resource is now protected in parks that contain Waimea Canyon, Kokee's upcountry forest, and the neighboring Alakai Swamp (the largest high-altitude swamp in the world), Polihale's beaches, and the incomparable coastline of mountains and valleys the Hawaiians called *na pali,* the cliffs. Credit must also be given to *kamaaina* families like the Robinsons for their commitment to maintaining Kauai's natural resources and spiritual integrity.

The result is a wilderness that attracts hikers to fabled trails, snorkelers and scuba divers to waters the color of melted aquamarines, and lures connoisseurs of the majestic into the air on helicopter tours or out to sea aboard a fleet of sailboats, catamarans, kayaks, and Zodiac rafts. Others are drawn by uncrowded beaches ranging from Poipu's crescents of

A warm smile at a plantation-town home.

Enjoying a shave ice at Haena, on the north shore.

6

Wailua Falls, one of many on the Garden Isle.

A windsurfer flies across north shore waters as storm clouds form overhead.

A pink dusk tints mountains and sea along Kauai's east coast.

The exotic flower of the passion fruit hangs on a Kokee forest vine.

Lavender water lilies blossom in a Garden Isle pond.

white sand to the golden miles that stretch from Hanalei to Haena. There are good reasons why Hawaiians peopled Kauai with spirits and gods and modern filmmakers have so often chosen it to represent paradise.

Change is already coming as word spreads of this most romantic, tropical, and isolated of Hawaii's main islands. At stake are the very pace and lifestyle that so perfectly complement the setting. Kauai exists in fragile balance, as many understand. With care, we can continue to enjoy this fragment of Eden known as Kauai.

Sunlight bursts through the branches of a flowering golden shower tree.

Birds of paradise are found in many backyard gardens.

Horses wander out to pasture at
Highgates' Ranch, upcountry Wailua.

An Island Is Formed

Four or five million years ago, a very different Kauai rose from the deep waters of the central Pacific. It was a barren island, still wearing the scars of ongoing volcanic activity. We do not know which other islands were neighbor to Kauai then. Oahu had already broken the surface of the sea, as perhaps had Molokai, but Lanai, Maui, Kahoolawe, and Hawaii had likely not yet begun to form on the ocean floor three miles below. Other high islands lay to the west. Today they are mere fragments of rock, coral atolls or underwater seamounts, trailing Kauai like a comet's tail more than 1,200 miles to Midway.

In the millions of years that saw these islands slowly sink back into the seabed, victims of their own great weight, Kauai also underwent change. From a once curving volcanic dome that peaked at between 8,000 and 10,000 feet, the storms of countless centuries have carved marvelous valleys and canyons that spiral from the center of the island and the towering rock walls of Mt. Waialeale.

Waialeale is all that remains of the crater through which Kauai's formative lavas flowed. At 5,148 feet it draws the clouds that deposit 450 inches of rain in an average year, making the summit one of the wettest places on earth. On days when it is free of clouds, you can see the sheer, hardrock walls of Waialeale's eastern face. Once they formed the center of the crater, but were exposed when a segment of its volcanic wall was blown away in an ancient cataclysmic explosion that reshaped the island.

By most estimates, it has been one to two million years since the Kauai volcano became extinct, its last series of eruptions having created the cinder cones and lowlands of south Kauai near Lihue, Koloa, and Poipu. But the forces of volcanic growth have long been overwhelmed by erosion: current estimates measure summit erosion at something like one foot every 2,500 years. The sea has also played a role, irresistibly tearing away at the integrity of the coastline, creating long expanses of beach from wave-shattered coral, and the towering seacliffs of the Na Pali coast. The sea has eroded the coastline at many different levels over the milennia as the climate changed and glaciers absorbed, released, and reabsorbed vast amounts of water from the encompassing Pacific.

The spires of the "Cathedral" reveal the erosive power of wind and rain along the storm-exposed Na Pali coast.

The relentless power of the sea has carved the Na Pali coast's rampart of cliffs.

Erosion isn't the only force at work, for like other aging volcanic islands, Kauai has begun to sink back into the seabed, its weight no longer supported by the magma reservoirs from which lava once flowed. According to current theory, these reservoirs are fed from the layer of liquid rock under the earth's drifting continental plates. Where these plates collide, great mountain ranges like the Himalayas and the Alaska Range are formed. Elsewhere, when one plate is pushed beneath another, it is drawn into the earth's molten interior where it melts, perhaps to be recycled in some future volcanic eruption. Kauai and the other Hawaiian islands, anchored to the Pacific plate, are thus being carried to the northwest, toward Japan and Asia.

The progress of these massive plates is often far from smooth. Earthquakes occur, releasing pent-up energy as the earth shifts along stretches of weakened fault lines. The Waimea River has carved its canyon by following the fault line

Lush forest surrounds Waialeale, remnant of the caldera of the Kauai volcano. A rare clear day reveals the 5,148-foot summit and the 3,000-foot walls of its eastern face.

Like Kauai's numerous other waterfalls, Opaekaa has played a role in eroding the Kauai landscape.

Kauai was formed by a single great volcano, which also created the neighboring island of Niihau. Current estimates are that it became extinct about one million years ago when it moved past the underground magma reservoirs that supplied it with lava.

known as the Makaweli Depression, its waters pulled seaward by gravity along the path of least resistance.

As the oldest of Hawaii's main islands, it is Kauai's monumentally sculpted beauty that most clearly differentiates the island from others of the archipelago. Only Oahu comes close to revealing a similar display of heavily eroded contours on the same immense scale. Only the oldest portions of the younger islands reveal what is everywhere evident on Kauai, where dramatic landscapes are emphasized by wilderness forests that trail the island's streams and grow on its near-vertical mountains. It is a landscape that has been a long time in the making. This lush mantle of green is perhaps the best reason for calling Kauai "the Garden Isle."

*Crashing surf near Poipu. Waves
have been dramatically reshaping
Kauai's coastline since the island
first emerged from the sea four or
five million years ago.*

A Lei Of Beaches

Beaches are a tribute to how well Kauai wears her age. Grain by grain they have accumulated over the span of perhaps a million years, formed by waves relentlessly attacking exposed coral reef and abandoned shells, leaving behind a trail of white and gold sands that are a signature of the Garden Isle. Some wind uninterrupted for miles, stitching the coast to a neon-brilliant sea. Others lie isolated, hidden between towering promontories or strung in crescents separated by headlands of lava rock. Storms, tides, and currents attack them, occasionally washing their sands away, only to redeposit them when calmer conditions prevail. It's a seasonal course of events, an inevitable part of the cycle of change that year by year alters the coastline, at times bringing destruction, at times regeneration.

All along the coast beaches provide ready access to the coral, crustaceans, and reef fish that prosper in warm, shallow waters, and to the abundance of deep, open seas lying just beyond. The ocean has historically provided sustenance for Kauai's people. Today, pleasure is as likely a lure, with sunbathers, beachcombers, swimmers, surfers, windsurfers, snorkelers, and divers sharing a still-uncrowded coastline.

The beauty of Kauai's beaches speaks for itself. From the isolated dunes and wide sands of Polihale that lie at the western edge of the dramatic Na Pali cliffs to Poipu's series of sheltered crescents in the south, from the resort-lined beaches between Hanamaulu and Kapaa in the east to the incomparable appeal of the north shore's miles of sandy coast, Kauai is a feast for the sunbather and water enthusiast, an island strung with a lei of magnificent beaches.

Kauai's beautiful beaches are a feast for sunbathers and water enthusiasts.

Sailors make a landing on Kalapaki Beach on Nawiliwili Bay.

Nearby mountains provide Kapaa Beach with a feel of the South Seas.

Uncrowded beaches mark the east coast from Hanamaulu to Kapaa.

A crescent beach fronts Poipu's neon waters.

*Crescents of sand and a turquoise sea,
at Lumahai Beach on the north shore.*

*Hanalei Bay and its mile
of curving beach.*

surfer checks out the waves at
ne of Poipu's string of beaches

A Zodiac raft carries passengers past the isolated beaches of the Na Pali coast.

The end of the day at the end of the road. Barking Sands Beach, west Kauai.

Reef-sheltered waters at Kee Beach cater to swimmers, snorkelers, and divers. This is where the north shore road ends and the Na Pali coast begins.

The Menehune

The goddess Pele and the demigod Maui are both linked to Kauai by Hawaiian belief and legend, but it is the elfin menehune who are most often associated with the Garden Isle. Shy forest dwellers, they were credited as master builders capable of completing major projects in a single night. The Alekoko Fishpond and the Menehune Ditch, an aquaduct that funnels water for irrigation from the Waimea River, were both attributed to their overnight efforts.

According to legend, the menehune worked at night so as not to be seen by others, cutting, transporting, and fitting the stones for their projects in a fireman's bucket brigade. If they were discovered their work would have to be abandoned. Luckily for the Hawaiians they served, the menehune were exceptionally good at remaining unnoticed.

Other legends tell how the menehune lived in caves in valleys like Wainiha, eating squash, starch pudding, sweet potato, and cooked taro leaves. They are said to have resisted mingling with the Hawaiians, fearful of diluting the purity of their race. In later times the Hawaiians counted them among their own ancestral spirits.

Today, scholars speculate that the menehune may not have been an imaginary race at all, but rather the descendants of the first wave of settlers who came to Hawaii from the Marquesas sometime around the sixth century. The menehune legends come from later settlers who reached Hawaii six or seven hundred years later from the islands of Tahiti. Scholars have concluded that this second wave of immigrants may have defeated the descendants of the original Marquesans, driving them north from the Big Island to Kauai, where they made their last stand. Only later did they emerge in their elfin guise. Linguistic support for the explanation comes from the Tahitian home islands where the word *manahune* derisively refer to a class of workers and slaves.

Whatever their origins, the menehune have emerged from the past as playful elves two or three feet tall, pot-bellied, hairy, and muscular, with bushy eyebrows over large eyes and a short thick nose with a trace of the mischievousness of their European counterparts. It is not impossible to believe that these ancients of Hawaiian belief still inhabit the moody forests of Kauai's deep interior.

The Menehune Fishpond is the most famous building project attributed to the menehune. As with all their endeavors, it was completed in one night.

The north shore's Wainiha Valley was a favorite with Kauai's menehune.

The menehune favor Kauai's deep forests, emerging to work only at night so as not to be seen.

Moonlight adds a mystic perspective to a Wainiha Valley stream.

An Island Apart

Kauai stands apart from the other main Hawaiian islands, too far from all but Niihau to be seen. More than 70 miles separate it from neighboring Oahu across the Kauai Channel. These are treacherous waters where strong winds and powerful currents often churn up the sea, forcing caution on passing ships.

Kamehameha learned that lesson in 1796 when, having added Maui, Molokai, Lanai, and Oahu to his dominions, he set out to complete his conquests by subduing Kauai. Departing from Oahu, his fleet of war canoes was swamped en route. Those that survived were forced to retreat to Oahu.

It would take Kamehameha six years to reassemble a fleet which by 1805 would include eight hundred newly built double-hulled war canoes and several European-style schooners. Kamehameha himself led the procession of ships as it made its way from the Big Island to Maui and then on to Oahu. There, while preparing for the final assault on Kauai, an epidemic of either typhoid or cholera devastated Kamehameha's forces again. Kauai was spared, its independence maintained.

The ultimate union of Kauai with the other islands under Kamehameha would take twenty years to accomplish. The slow, if inevitable, process began in 1810, when Kauai's King Kaumualii sailed to Oahu aboard an American trade ship to meet with Kamehameha. At the royal compound the negotiations began, bringing through diplomacy what had eluded Kamehameha in war when Kaumualii accepted Kamehameha's protection, returning to Kauai to rule as a tributary king.

The pact would be renewed in 1821 when Kaumualii again surrendered his sovereignty, this time to a less-trusting Kamehameha II, who brought Kaumualii with him to Honolulu where he was forced to live out the last years of his life as proof of his loyalty. Kaahumanu, the widowed queen Kamehameha had named as regent on his death, went one step further in securing Kauai's tacit surrender by marrying both Kaumualii and his son, the handsome Prince Kealiiahonui.

The final attempt to assert Kauai's independence followed Kaumualii's death in 1824, when he willed Kauai and Niihau to the Kamehamehas rather than to his oldest son. Spurred on by tradition, Kauai's chiefs rallied around the heir to the throne, Kaumualii's son George. It proved a short-lived rebellion, the last gasp of a dying age, and when it was over Kauai was no longer an island apart, but an integral part of the Hawaiian Kingdom.

Westernmost of the major Hawaiian islands, Kauai can only be seen from Niihau. Remote from the other islands of the Hawaiian chain, Kauai has a distinct sense of isolation.

Kamehameha's paddling warriors were twice forced to abandon plans to conquer Kauai. Their first effort in 1796 was turned back by rough seas that capsized a portion of the fleet. The second attempt in 1805 was cancelled when a typhoid epidemic devastated Kamehameha's forces as they prepared to attack Kauai with a fleet of 800 war canoes. The island was not officially incorporated into the Hawaiian Kingdom until 1824 when it was willed to the Kamehamehas by Kaumualii, last king of Kauai.

A wave crests in the dangerous waters of the wide and often treacherous channel separating Kauai from neighboring Oahu. Surrounding seas have traditionally served as a buffer between Kauai and the other Hawaiian islands.

The ruins of a heiau to Laka, goddess of hula, overlook Kee Beach and the sea.

Captain Cook and officers from HMS Resolution and HMS Discovery are treated to roast pig outside a priest's house. The Kauaians accepted Cook as the god Lono when he landed in Waimea. His arrival seemed to fulfill the prophecy that Lono would return to Hawaii on floating islands from across the sea. Expedition artist John Webber recorded this scene and others that trace the people, places, and events of Cook's third Pacific voyage, 1776-1780.

Captain Cook

RENDEZVOUS WITH HISTORY

While the Polynesians had known of Hawaii since the sixth century, it was not until the end of the eighteenth century that Europe would make its discovery. As dawn broke on the morning of January 18, 1778, Captain James Cook weighed anchor in reef-sheltered waters off the village of Waimea on Kauai.

Hawaiian legends had told of the return of the god Lono from across the sea. When Cook and his high-masted ships, the *Discovery* and the *Resolution,* sailed into view, they matched legendary descriptions of the god's return on strange floating islands. In the context of the times it is not surprising that the Hawaiians mistook Cook for Lono and his crew of pipe-smoking sailors as his fire-breathing retainers. The misconception was reinforced by Cook's refined manner and his awareness of native sensitivities gained in earlier visits to Tahiti, the Marquesas, and other Polynesian islands of the South Pacific. Cook was quick to see the similarities between the Hawaiians and these other islanders, as he would note later that day in the ship's log:

"At this time we were in some doubt whether or not the land before us was inhabited, this doubt was soon cleared up by seeing some canoes coming off from the shore towards the ships. I immediately brought to to give them time to come up, there were three or four men in each and we were agreeably surprised to find them of the same nation as the people of Otaheiti [Tahiti] and the other islands we had lately visited."

That observation was later confirmed and elaborated on by James King, captain of the *Discovery:* "What more than all surprised us was our catching the sound of Otaheiti words in their speech, and on asking them for hogs, breadfruit, yams, in that dialect, we found we were understood, and that these were in plenty on shore."

The surprise was no less great for the villagers. As Cook would later observe: "I never saw Indians [as all native people had come to be called] so much astonished at entering a ship before, their eyes were continually flying from object to object, the wildness of their looks and actions fully expressed their surprise and astonishment at the several new objects before them and evinced that they never had been on board a ship before."

Good intentions, however, were not enough and before Cook had departed Kauai, the first Hawaiian had been killed in a shorefront confrontation with a small landing party sent out to search for water. It was the first of numerous misunderstandings that would mark the meetings between the Hawaiians and the foreigners (*haoles*) who soon made their way to the islands.

Unapprised of this incident, Cook went ashore the following day and was immediately surrounded by hundreds of natives

COURTESY ANCESTRAL ARTS GALLERY, HONOLULU

from a heavily populated beachfront village. They immediately fell to the ground, pressing their faces to the earth in an expression of deep respect reserved for the highest *alii* (royalty). A ceremony followed, with Cook gifted of several small pigs.

Returning to shore the next day to barter iron and trinkets for fresh water and food, Cook was soon escorted by a *kahuna* (priest) to a nearby *heiau* (temple). En route they passed irrigated fields of taro, sugarcane, sweet potatoes, and other crops. The temple consisted of an enclosed rock platform housing several buildings and numerous carved *tiki* (god images), several of which were clothed in bark cloth called tapa. There were also the graves of at least ten chiefs within the compound, the *mana* (spiritual power) of their bones providing powerful links to the gods. For this reason the remains of the dead were held sacred and were carefully protected from theft and spiritual misuse by enemies.

Central to the heiau was a tall oracle tower, its platforms used for various rituals. Offerings to the gods were placed on the lowest platform, special ceremonies were performed on the second, while the highest platform was reserved for use by the ruling chief and the temple priests. It was here, through them, that the gods spoke. The freedom with which Cook and his men were allowed to wander about the normally *kapu* (forbidden) precincts of the heiau was another sign of the special courtesy shown Cook as the returning Lono.

High surf and a threatening storm soon set Cook searching for a safer anchorage than that offered by Waimea. When nothing more promising could be found along the Kauai coast, the *Discovery* and *Resolution* set a westward course in search of new islands. None would be found until the following year when, after a summer spent searching for a northern passage linking the Atlantic and Pacific, Cook returned to the tropics for provisions and came upon Maui, Molokai, Lanai, and Hawaii.

Though Cook's visit to Kauai had lasted less than two weeks, history had nonetheless been made. For better or worse the outside world now knew of Hawaii and the Hawaiians of the outside world. For these islands, strategically located in the heart of the Pacific, things would never be the same.

COURTESY NATIONAL GALLERY OF NEW ZEALAND, WELLINGTON

Captain James Cook, greatest of Europe's eighteenth-century explorers, traversed the Pacific on three extended voyages of discovery. He was killed in 1779 on the island of Hawaii after a tragic misunderstanding between his men and the native Hawaiians.

The Kauai village of Waimea in 1778 in a Webber watercolor. It was here that Cook made his first landfall in the Hawaiian Islands. Note the casks for resupplying the ships with fresh water, the crewmen trading with the villagers, and the feather cape of royalty on the figure left of center.

COURTESY LIBRARY OF NEW SOUTH WALES, SYDNEY, AUSTRALIA

reconstructed oracle tower at
mokila Hawaiian Village on the
ilua River. It was on the three
tforms of the oracle tower that
erings were made and that the
ests and ruling chief communi-
ed with the gods.

Images of gods draped in
white tapa (bark cloth) in a
heiau at Waimea, Kauai, are
recorded in this 1778
Webber watercolor.

Niihau

THE FORBIDDEN ISLAND

On most days you can see Niihau from coastal Kekaha or from the winding upcountry road that leads to Waimea Canyon and Kokee. Square edged and mysterious, Niihau is isolated by geography and circumstance, for the entire island belongs to Kauai's Robinson family, and they have chosen to maintain Niihau as an outpost of traditional Hawaii rather than open it to the pressures of the outside world.

Seventeen miles southwest of Kauai, this 72 square miles of low-lying volcanic real estate is home to over two hundred pure-blooded Hawaiians. It is the preserve of a world that is no more. Hawaiian is spoken, and the way of life harkens back to that of more than a century ago when the island was purchased by Elizabeth Sinclair from Kamehameha V for $10,000. That was in 1864, and since that time Niihau has been kept Hawaiian by the efforts of Sinclair and her descendants.

Dry and semi-barren, Niihau was built by the same volcano that created Kauai. When sea levels were lower at the height of the last ice age, the two were very likely one island. With rain-bearing clouds blocked by towering Waialeale, Niihau is usually clear of cloud cover and rain. It's only 1,281 feet to the island's summit at Paniau, and that's not enough to attract clouds or moisture to what has come to be called "the Forbidden Island."

Fishing and cultivating taro were the traditional occupations on Niihau. Ranching was introduced only after Sinclair's purchase, and ever since, one animal or another has grazed the island's often meager pastures. The lifestyle follows the tempo and technology of the past. Homes are lit by kerosene lamps, for with the exception of a generator or two there is no electricity. There are no telephones either, for communication is via shortwave radio, nor is there a need for paved roads or traffic lights, for a few ranch trucks are the island's only motorized vehicles.

Niihau's residents turn to Kauai for supplies and the services of the outside world. This is where high school-age students go to school, usually boarding with relatives or friends in the spirit of *ohana* (extended family) that remains a fundamental part of Hawaiian tradition.

While an occasional flight makes use of Niihau's small airstrip, access is usually by boat. But don't expect a big lei

The Kaulakahi Channel and the island of Niihau as seen from Kekaha, Kauai.

greeting unless you've been invited by a resident and approved by the ranch that still operates there. For all others, Niihau remains off limits, at once a mystery and an anachronism. No one denies that the system is rigid, but it is designed to protect a consciousness and a way of life, and thus is widely supported. At a time when modernization and development have transformed the unique into the anonymous, Niihau is indeed a remarkable place, a mystery seen by most only at a distance.

On some days it rises clearly from above Kekaha's canefields and the white-capped blues of the channel that separates it from Kauai. From the air it lies aligned like a distant extension of the Na Pali coast, while the sunset burns it into sharp silhouette against an orange sky.

Then there are the days when clouds or mist hide Niihau from view. Looking toward the western horizon, nothing appears where Niihau should be. On such days, with invisibility as a cover, the sense of mystery that surrounds Niihau, Hawaii's Forbidden Isle, is all the more complete.

The elegance of the hula is enhanced by leis of delicate Niihau shells.

An eighteenth-century view of Niihau, or O'nee-how, as it was then called.

Leis of Niihau shells. The highly valued shells are found only on the beaches of the Forbidden isle.

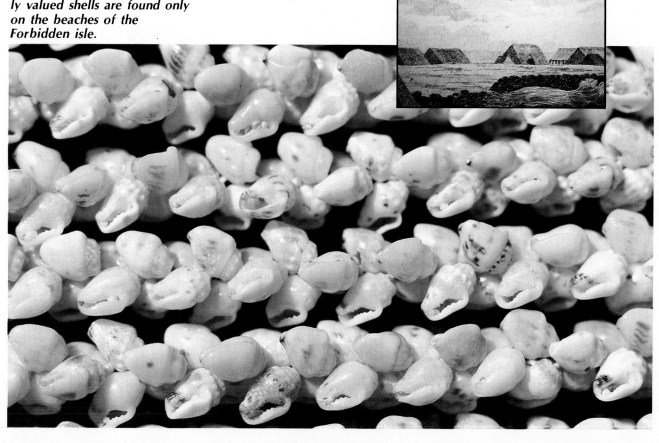

The sun sets over the
Kaulakahi Channel and Niihau.

Waimea Canyon

From the lookouts on its western rim the stream that has carved Waimea Canyon is barely visible. No sound of rushing water pierces the thousands of feet of silence that separate it from those standing above. The curving fragments of river that are revealed require discovery, as do the wild goats that forage the canyon's ridges or the waterfalls that hide in the creases of the canyon's vertical walls.

From above, the primordial earth lies exposed by more than a million years of erosion. On a sunny day, when luminous clouds pass overhead and are reflected in shadows traced on the canyon walls, color rushes at you in everchanging variations of orange and pink, purple and green. On other days, when colors are dulled by steely-grey mists or when columns of rain race across the canyon on their way from Waialeale to the sea, the grand view is replaced by subtlety and attention to detail.

From within, the canyon is also subtly defined, but in the details of personal experience. The confining nature of its towering walls, the flow of water as it courses between the rocks and boulders of the streambed, the sharp-edged notes of songbirds hidden in a leafy canopy of forest are aspects of its style, focusing attention on the immediacy of the moment. From within, new perspectives are gained on what Mark Twain aptly called the Grand Canyon of the Pacific.

Both day and night have their own meaning on the canyon floor. It's not until a few hours after sunrise that the sun finally crosses the canyon's eastern rim, so daylight is preceded by a long dawn. Dew hangs heavily on tall grasses and spider webs as the day begins. Reflections of the sunlit cliffs above shine in still-shaded pools, adding depth and color.

A pale-blue sky deepens as the day wears on and dawn's chill surrenders to midday's warmth. Stream-fed pools offer cool relief from the increasing heat, with water rushing past like cool, thick air. Boulders midstream provide a place for warming up surrounded by the crackling of running water and the sound of kukui and guava trees brushed by a passing breeze.

From deep within the canyon the setting sun toys with the serrated edge of the towering western rim. The evening is preceded by a dusk made long by the sun's early departure. When daylight finally fades, night locks the canyon in near-total blackness. Sound replaces sight in confirming the existence of an outside world. A rough scraping of the earth reveals a wild boar foraging for food. In the dense forest of the canyon floor few stars penetrate the canopy of leaves that by day are irridescent with sunlight.

But the forces of nature are not always so benevolent in their carving of this canyon. There are also times when storms determine the flow of river, and then the spectacle is considerably different. When grey skies hang low and heavy in the sky, the quiet is replaced by pelting rains and winds that set the canyon's trees to creaking. In a single day a dozen storms may pass, usually rolling in from the east, where Waialeale's heights draw rain from encompassing clouds.

The days when rains are particularly strong and the buildup of water from the highlands comes too quickly, the steady flow of the canyon's stream is replaced by the surging power of a flash flood. Set to lightning's electric flash and the echo of thunder off the canyon walls, the Waimea stream is then transformed into a mud-brown wall of water that races through the canyon, carrying with it the debris of rain-carved landslides, trees fro the shoreline forests, and great boulders from the streambed. Within minutes waters can rise 15 to 20 feet, turbulently scouring the canyon floor, carving new contours that might otherwise have taken years to accomplish.

The rain-swollen waters of Waimea stream are transformed into a thick flow of watery mud as a flash flood rushes downstream.

The sun sets over the canyon's west rim.

A hiker crosses one of several hanging bridges over Waimea stream as it winds its way from the heart of the canyon to the sea.

The colorful spectacle of Waimea Canyon from a canyon-rim lookout.

From within, the canyon also reveals secrets of other times. Abandoned houses and small dams tell of the past use made of the canyon's waters for irrigation. Water is still diverted from the lower reaches of the canyon, channeled in sluices to the thirsty canefields of the lowlands.

Other secrets of a more mystical nature may also be revealed, particularly on nights when the moon is full and the canyon is filled with a luminous glow. It is then, in the canyon's deserted depths, that times long gone by echo from a past when these islands were Polynesian and unaware of the rest of the world. Many stories are told of just such moments by those who have spent time within Waimea's towering walls: the stories tell of beating drums and ancient spirits. Like the layered canyon walls that erosion has unveiled, they are a reflection of the past and of the powerful forces that still shape Waimea canyon today.

A rainbow stretches over a vast canyon gorge.

South Kauai

THE LANDSCAPED LOWLANDS

The fertile soil of Kauai's expansive southern lowlands has provided an agricultural base since Polynesian times when yams, sweet potatoes, taro, coconuts, sugarcane, and breadfruit were part of the harvest. Villages of steep-roofed *hales* (houses) made of rock and wood covered in dried grasses or leaves were clustered along the coast, along streams that provided water for taro, or in the cooler hills upcountry. *Heiaus* (temples) built to the gods, such as those found at Poliahu on the Wailua River, still survive. Among them is one of the oldest in Hawaii, for the inviting south coast was an early homeland for the Polynesians who settled these islands.

The nineteenth century brought with it a whole new way of life, as sugar was planted by the tens of thousands of acres and cane gave Kauai a plantation lifestyle and a Japanese and Filipino population to replace the dwindling number of native Hawaiians. It was here on the fields of south Kauai that plantation agriculture got its start with the opening of the Koloa Plantation and mill in 1835.

In the decades that followed, other plantations would be established all along the south coast. Lihue, Kauai's largest town and county seat, opened its first mill in 1849, adding the Hanamaulu Plantation within a few years. By the 1860s canefields stretched for more than 30 miles, rolling across the countryside from Kapaa in the east to Kekaha in the west.

The Lihue and Koloa plantations would prove to be pace-setters for Hawaii's sugar industry. The plan for Koloa, with its mills, schools, churches, and stores, was a blueprint for the great plantations that would emerge by the 1860s on all of the islands. Koloa's workers received housing, medical care, a ration of fish and poi, and one *hapawalu* (12½ cents) in plantation money for a day's work. This "Kauai money," issued because the kingdom had not yet established its own currency, could be used to buy goods at the plantation store.

By the 1850s, Lihue Plantation had taken the lead from Koloa, introducing irrigation with the building of a network of tunnels and channels that brought water from the mountains and carried it to the dry fields of the south coast. In 1853 the plantation could boast Hawaii's first steam-operated mill. Within ten years the landscape would be dotted with neatly laid out, self-contained plantation towns, all smelling of molasses and dominated by the mill, where cane was crushed and sugar extracted.

Today, while cane still covers the landscape in vibrant green, the work of refining is handled by only a few mills, with future prospects clouded by failing profits. There is indeed a chance that within the foreseeable future more than 150 years of plantation agriculture may be little more than an historical interlude.

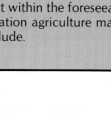

Canefields on either side, a school bus heads toward the Koloa Mill near Poipu. The Koloa Plantation is Hawaii's oldest, having opened in 1835. INSET: The Koloa Plantation in the nineteenth century.

HAWAII STATE ARCHIVES

That would be an unfortunate loss, for sugar has provided more than an economic base: it has also preserved a rural pace and the broad, cluttered vistas in keeping with Kauai's natural beauty. South Kauai's small towns reveal the fragile nature of what has almost anachronistically been preserved, with Hanapepe, Waimea, Koloa, Kapaa, and Lihue each retaining a sense of small-town familiarity and the feel of simpler, less pressured times.

If agriculture is on the wane, tourism is not, and it is along the south and east coasts that resorts have sprung up over the past decade, taking advantage of clear, sunny skies, many miles of beach, and warm, reef-lined waters. Separated by coastal lowlands from the mountains that attract clouds and supply the north of the island with abundant rains, the southern half of Kauai is generally dry, with a climate similar to that of Waikiki.

It's not surprising to find that hotels and condominiums from Poipu to Lihue (Kalapaki Beach), from Hanamaulu to Wailua and Kapaa, lure the lion's share of Kauai's annual crop of visitors. Golf, tennis, horseback riding, helicopter touring, plus historic and cultural attractions like the Grove Farm homestead, Old Koloa Town with its charming cluster of shops, and the Lihue Museum add to obvious assets of setting, climate, and the floral wonders of south Kauai's botanical gardens and nurseries.

Water sports play a key role in the popularity of the south coast. Poipu's surf often attracts Kauai's best surfers, while others take to more familiar pursuits like sailing or windsurfing. The Kapaa coast also provides some excellent windsurfing opportunities, and along with Poipu, some very appealing reefs frequented by divers and snorkelers. Rafts, catamarans, sailboats, sportfishing boats, and other pleasure craft depart Koloa Landing (where whalers once laid anchor), Nawiliwili harbor (Lihue's port), and Kalapaki Beach with its resort.

And there is more, for south Kauai's horn of plenty also spills forth waterfalls like Wailua and Opaekaa, visited by long-tailed tropic birds; lavatube blowholes like Poipu's Spouting Horn, which shoots sea spray 50 feet into the air; lush valleys like Hanapepe; and the popular streamside Fern Grotto.

A tunnel of giant eucalyptus trees nearly a mile long shades the road to Koloa and Poipu.

New shops and restaurants have brought a revival to the old sugar town of Koloa, which now serves as a commercial hub for nearby Poipu resorts.

The Spouting Horn lava tube creates ocean spray geysers of up to 50 feet.

Kalapaki Beach and its adjacent Westin resort face Nawiliwili Harbor and south Kauai's Hoary Head mountains.

Snorkelers enjoy the south co warm, reef-sheltered wa

*illian Leihulu Kaui says
loha with a warm
awaiian smile.*

*A Poipu sunset accentuates
Kauai's tropical mood.*

*Lihue, Kauai's largest town and
county seat, retains the feel of a
plantation town. Lihue's mill is one
of four still operating on Kauai.*

The grotto lies several miles upstream from where the Wailua River meets the sea. This is Hawaii's largest permanent river, draining the island's central core of mountains and the surrounding coastal lowlands. The cruise boats that depart the Wailua Marina are the only access to the grotto, providing Hawaiian entertainment and history en route, plus a musical serenade, Hawaiian-style, once you've arrived.

The remains of several heiaus, some partially restored, reveal the spiritual importance of this part of the Garden Isle in Polynesian times. It was here, in an isolated compound, that many of Kauai's chiefs were born, and here that Kauai's largest place of refuge *(puuhonua)* was located.

Several centuries later, planters would take advantage of the beneficial mix of sunlight and abundant water to establish Hawaii's largest palm grove to produce copra. Today thousands of swaying palms are all that remain of that venture, providing the Coco Palms and the Coconut Plantation resorts with an appealingly tropical ambience, matched by a winding stretch of beach and reef-lined seas. Several state parks in the area provide riverside or oceanfront locales for picnics or a swim.

On an island made for relaxation, this is also a perfect place to sit back and do little more than contemplate the path of falling coconuts or appreciate the contrast of palms against the colors of the setting sun or a dusk sky. Here, where the landscape flows in a lush procession of color, and fresh, fragrant breezes frequently blow in from the mountains or from over the sea, the landscaped beauty of Kauai's southern lowlands is exquisitely revealed.

A serenade at the Fern Grotto.

Flat-bottom riverboats make their way up the Wailua River to the grotto throughout the day.

Magic & Beauty On The North Shore

There is no place in Hawaii where beauty and magic seem so close to merging as along Kauai's north shore. Even as you're approaching, panoramas come into view, with distant mountains rising from a fertile plateau that's been in pasture for more than a century. Justifiably contented cows, calves, and horses graze their way across thousands of acres of the Princeville Ranch.

Named in honor of a 1860 visit paid by King Kamehameha IV, Queen Emma, and their son Albert Edward Kauikeaouli, the Prince of Hawaii, Princeville was then a sugar plantation. The great joy at the birth of an heir to the throne, acknowledged in the choice of Princeville's name, soon turned to sorrow, however, for this last child born to any Hawaiian monarch would die soon after his fourth birthday.

Today, ranching and resort development share Princeville's 11,000 acres, with golf, tennis, and poolside lounging offered from a dramatic clifftop setting with a rampart of green mountains and the perfect crescent of Hanalei Bay as a backdrop. It's an addictive view, peaceful in the way of nature at its most inspiring, a soft-edged place that caresses with breezes, showers, tropical fragrances, ten curving miles of uncrowded beaches, and a sea of stained-glass hues.

It is the sea that gave Hanalei its name (*hana:* bay; *lei:* wreath, crescent). Along with the catches it provided fishermen, it also linked the north shore to the outside world. By the 1830s, Protestant missionaries had already settled and built the Waioli Mission, converting the Hawaiians and training them in religious and secular ways. Whalers came soon after, reprovisioning their ships from the 1840s to the 1860s. Then livestock and crops ranging from rice to taro were exported on inter-island steamers. Now pleasure craft and fishermen head out over the reef at the mouth of the bay to reach the open sea and the fishing, snorkeling, and adventure of the nearby Na Pali coast.

The eight coastal miles that link Hanalei and this empire of jagged cliffs (*na pali:* the cliffs) only emphasize Hanalei's beauty and appeal. This is the primal landscape of tropic dreams, where monuments of volcanic rock draped in a lush forest of green meet the sea in beaches overhung by ironwood and palm. Hollywood has unveiled this stretch of coast in many guises over the years. *South Pacific, King Kong,* and *The Thornbirds* are some of the movies in which the north shore has played the south seas.

Helicopter tours provide magnificent views of the exquisite Na Pali coast.

That the reality of the north shore is every bit as intense as its movie roles explains why Hawaiians people these forested valleys and the wet and dry caves along the coast with menehune, spirits, and gods. On a hillside overlooking Kee Beach and the Na Pali's long line of seacliffs, they also built a temple to Laka, the goddess of hula.

Today the partially restored temple shares its timeless setting with swimmers, hikers, snorkelers, and a small armada of boats and rafts, emphasizing just how much has changed. The wilderness that now begins with the first of the Na Pali cliffs was once heavily populated. Now only a few hikers trek the 11 cliffside miles of the ancient Kalalau trail. Thousands once lived along this coast, harvesting taro from terraced fields that followed streambeds to the backs of great valleys like Hanakapiai, Kalalau, and Honopu. An aerial tour reveals the outlines of housesites and terraces, still quite evident despite the passing of more than a century since they were last cultivated.

Princeville offers the finest in golf, horseback riding and tennis.

Kalalau Valley from a lookout 4,000 feet above sea level in Kokee State Park.

DAVID CORNWELL

Hanalei Valley's taro fields.
The valley is protected as a
bird refuge, home to rare
Hawaiian stilts and more com-
mon cattle egrets.

A taro farmer harvests
his crop. Hanalei Valley.

Hanalei resident Louise Marsten carries the pride of her Polynesian heritage.

Despite growth, Hanalei has retained much of its rural charm.

Hanalei Bay from the Princeville Resort.

In the silent wilderness that now prevails it seems hard to imagine living in such an awesome, isolated setting, pressed to the sea by sheer valley walls rising 3,000 to 4,000 feet in spired pinnacles and knife-edged ridges. Rainbows, waterfalls, crashing waves, hypnotic sunsets, and misting storms explain why those who come here today pay homage to the beauty of this coast.

If Kauai is a garden isle, then the north shore is its crowning glory, a score of miles that sets fantasies in motion, hearts at peace. It is easy to believe simple truths when you pass this way, easy to surrender to the casual pace, cautious smiles, and the feel of different standards, different times. When a fragile mist paints vibrant rainbows that seem close enough to touch or storm clouds darken the afternoon sky, when waterfalls follow the rains that keep things so abundantly green or the setting sun outlines Bali Hai in stark silhouette, then it's also easy to see how beauty and magic have merged here on Kauai's north shore.

Hanakapiai, two miles in from the Kalalau trailhead near Kee Beach, was the last of the Na Pali coast valleys to maintain a native Hawaiian community. By the 1930s, the coastal valleys were all deserted.

Lumahai Beach is one of the most photogenic in Hawaii.

Sunset, Bali Hai, near the start of the Na Pali coast.